Around the World

Clothes Around the World

By Meg Gaertner

level 2 little blue readers

www.littlebluehousebooks.com

Little Blue House is distributed by North Star Editions:
sales@northstareditions.com | 888-417-0195

Produced for Little Blue House by Red Line Editorial.

Photographs ©: iStockphoto, cover, 7, 10, 13, 16, 18–19, 21, 22–23, 24 (top left), 24 (top right), 24 (bottom left), 24 (bottom right); Shutterstock Images, 4, 8–9, 14–15

Library of Congress Control Number: 2020900818

ISBN
978-1-64619-182-6 (hardcover)
978-1-64619-216-8 (paperback)
978-1-64619-284-7 (ebook pdf)
978-1-64619-250-2 (hosted ebook)

Printed in the United States of America
Mankato, MN
082020

About the Author

Meg Gaertner enjoys reading, writing, dancing, and being outside. She lives in Minnesota, where she has to wear very warm clothes in the winter.

Table of Contents

Many Types

People around the world wear different kinds of clothes.

This woman covers her face.

You can still see her eyes.

These men wear thick clothes. Thick clothes keep them warm.

blanket

Bright Colors

This person wears
a blanket.
The blanket is colorful.

These women wear cloth.

The cloth is colorful.

cloth

These boys wear ponchos. The ponchos have many colors.

poncho

Dressing Up

These children are in a parade. They dress up in nice clothing.

These people dress up in robes.
They wear belts.

robe
belt

These women dress up in beads.

It is an important day.

beads

This woman dresses up
in a big skirt.
A big skirt is good
for dancing.

skirt

Glossary

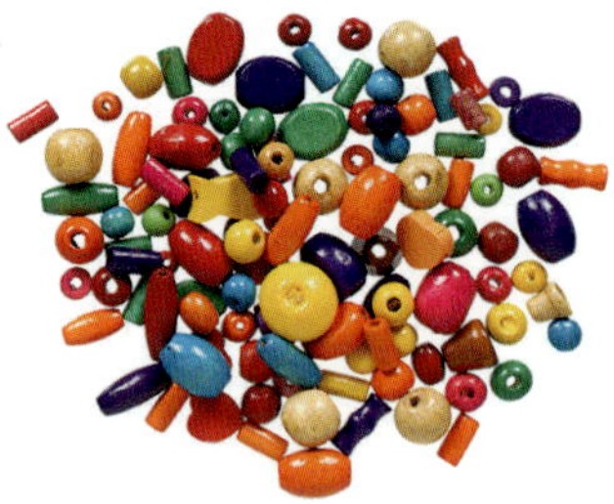

beads

blanket

belt

skirt

Index